# THE
# TITHING
## CONSPIRACY

Exposing the Lies & False Teachings
About Tithing and the Prosperity Gospel

TERRENCE JAMESON

Copyright © 2016 by Terrence Jameson. All rights reserved.

Inspired Word Publishers

*Printed in the United States of America*

No part of this book may be reproduced in any written, electronic, recording, or photocopying without written permission of the publisher or author.

All Bible quotations are taken from the King James Version except where indicated.

Scripture taken from *The Message*. Copyright © 1993, 1994, 1995, 1996, 2000, 2001, 2002. Used by permission of NavPress Publishing Group.

THE HOLY BIBLE, NEW INTERNATIONAL VERSION®, NIV® Copyright © 1973, 1978, 1984, 2011 by Biblica, Inc.® Used by permission. All rights reserved worldwide.

Scripture taken from the New King James Version®. Copyright © 1982 by Thomas Nelson. Used by permission. All rights reserved.

Scripture quotations marked (NLT) are taken from the Holy Bible, New Living Translation, copyright © 1996, 2004, 2007 by Tyndale House Foundation. Used by permission of Tyndale House Publishers, Inc., Carol Stream, Illinois 60188. All rights reserved.

Scripture quotations are from the New Revised Standard Version Bible, copyright © 1989 the Division of Christian Education of the National Council of the Churches of Christ in the United States of America. Used by permission. All rights reserved.

ISBN-13: 978-0692613672
ISBN-10: 0692613676

TheTithingConspiracy.com

TerrenceJameson.com

## Table of Contents

Introduction ................................................................. 1
Chapter 1. Why Are You Being Lied To?............................... 5
Chapter 2. When Did Tithing Begin?.................................... 11
Chapter 3. Who Has the Right To Receive Tithe? .................. 25
Chapter 4. Who Was Really Cursed in Malachi 3:9?.............. 29
Chapter 5. Why Should You Continue Giving?...................... 35
Chapter 6. How Do You Financially Support a Church Organization ... 43

# Introduction

One day while riding the Metrorail, I saw a Jewish man seated a few rows ahead of me. Anxious to know more about how Jews viewed tithing, I gathered the courage to go up to him and ask a question.

I said, "Excuse me, sir. Do Jews still tithe?"

He gave me a bewildered look, so I asked him the question a bit differently.

"Excuse me, sir. I was doing some research on tithing, and I would like to know if Jews still tithe."

He replied, "No. Jews no longer tithe because the temple has been destroyed. But if the temple were rebuilt, Jews would have to resume tithing."

I asked him, "If Jews no longer tithe, how are your religious activities supported?"

He said, "Members support their synagogue with offerings because only priests are allowed to receive tithe. Furthermore, tracing one's ancestry back to Aaron is next to impossible because of the diaspora, so this presents a problem with tithing. Also, in present times, supporting synagogues with grain and sheep is impractical because we no longer live in an agricultural society."

Wow! The Jews no longer hold tithing as a present-day requirement. I knew that tithing began with the Jews, so their views on tithing and its continued use were very important. Why? Paul answers this question: *"What advantage then hath the Jew?...Much in every way: chiefly, because that unto them were committed the oracles of God"* (Romans 3:1-2). Additionally, the first Christians were Jews!

With that brief conversation, I received an answer to almost all my tithing questions. But why was I asking questions about tithing?

I was raised in a Christian denomination that teaches tithing, and I did not question or challenge my denomination's beliefs on tithing. I knew God instructed Moses to establish the tithing system because Levites were not included in the inheritance in the Promised Land. I understood that the other eleven tribes brought 10 percent of their increase to the temple, and this helped meet the basic needs of the priests and Levites living among them. I assumed, like during the time when Moses lived, tithing was needed to support people that dedicate their lives to God and the ministry.

I was 30 years old before I began to seriously question tithing. At the time, I was attending a very prominent church in Virginia whose membership was mostly upper-middle class. I was new to the area and discovered very quickly that northern Virginia was an expensive place to live. I was underemployed at the time, and like many people living in the area, I needed a roommate to afford a decent apartment. Paying tithe coupled with high living expenses, put a tremendous strain on my finances.

My mother was unemployed and having a hard time paying her bills. I had very little money, but I sent her what little I had after paying my own expenses. This went on for a few months. I was giving 10 percent of my income to the church, paying my bills, and giving my mother whatever I had left, which was not enough to meet her financial obligations. This did not seem right.

I asked myself, "Does the church need the money more than my mother?"

It certainly did not seem that way. The church I attended ran two services and collected approximately $40,000 - $60,000 a week from the second service alone. The church was in a nice building, in a good neighborhood, and had more than enough money to pay the salaries of staff (janitors, musicians, secretaries, etc.) and five pastors. The paltry amount that I paid in tithe was insignificant to the church's overall income. However, I could see how giving that money to my mother would help her pay her bills, keep the collection agencies from calling, and her home from foreclosure. I began to question whether I was disobeying the fifth commandment that says: _"Honor thy father and thy mother"_ *(Exodus*

*20:12)*, and doing what Jesus scolded the Pharisees for doing; failing to financially support their parents by giving their money to the synagogue when he said: *"Why do you break the command of God for the sake of your tradition? For God said, 'Honor your father and mother' and 'Anyone who curses their father or mother is to be put to death.' But you say that if anyone declares that what might have been used to help their father or mother is 'devoted to God,' they are not to 'honor their father or mother' with it. Thus you nullify the word of God for the sake of your tradition."* (NIV, Matthew 15:3-6).

I decided to give the money I paid in tithe to my mother. However, my spirit was uncomfortable with this, and I wondered if I had made the right decision. I was raised to believe that you must give God his portion first, and I feared for my financial security. I seriously believed that my income would be cursed by this but was willing to take the risk. My mother needed help. To my surprise, my financial situation did not improve or get any worse.

After the conversation with the Jewish man on the train, the burden I was carrying was released. I could now support my mother financially without feeling guilty about not returning God his tithe. However, with this new knowledge came more questions. Why and how did the Old Testament tithing system change to what we see today? Do Christians know that Jews no longer tithe? How many people presently feel the way I was feeling? I knew more people needed to understand tithing.

More than ten years after that eventful train ride, I decided to write this book to educate, teach, and expose the lies and false teachings about tithing and the prosperity gospel. My objective is to free you from the pressure, shame, guilt, condemnation, and social stigma that come from not paying tithes. In each chapter, you will discover and learn biblical facts 100% backed by scripture that proves that tithing has never been a Christian obligation.

The purpose of this book is not to convince you to stop giving to your local church or whatever religious organization you support! There are numerous reasons why you should continue giving. The goal of this writing is to educate and dispel the pernicious lies and false teachings about a Jewish system that is not required by Christians.

# Chapter 1

## Why Are You Being Lied To?

Religion, not to be confused with Christianity, is a sold commodity in the United States and many parts of the world. Religion has become a multi-billion dollar industry that attracts profit-seeking entrepreneurs. Despite the extensive competition to attract parishioners, the barriers to entry are small, and the start-up costs are relatively low. In most cases, you do not need an advanced degree, significant start-up capital, or prior experience. Turning a small congregation into a megachurch (a church having 2,000 or more people in average weekend attendance) has often been one of the easiest and fastest get rich quick schemes in the world. To attract thousands of followers, all that is generally needed is confidence, a good speaking voice, above-average presentation skills, a general understanding of the Bible, and a prosperity message that makes people believe that if you attend their church regularly and are faithful in paying your tithe, riches and wealth is within their reach. Contrast this prosperity message with a church where the focus is on teaching members to practice the lifestyle of Jesus Christ, which is centered on forgiveness, love, charity, and servant leadership, and you easily recognize the difference.

Success does not have to equal the prosperity preaching TV evangelists. Many of these pastors wear tailored suits, own expensive cars, travel in private airplanes purchased with their church's money, and live in million-dollar mansions. For every one of these prosperity preachers that have achieved an extraordinary level of financial success, there are many other less successful preachers robbing their congregation(s). Just like their more successful counterparts, their philosophy is why work a 9 to 5 job to make a living when it is much easier and far more lucrative to convince others to give you money.

In order for prosperity preachers to convince people to give them money, they must make it appear they are faithful pastors that have committed their lives to preach the gospel. However, if you carefully study their message and listen to their sermons' repetitive tone, it won't be long before you discover their message is based on tithing to achieve prosperity; you have to give in order to get. You will often hear them say it is God's desire for you to have a more abundant and prosperous life, but your attitude and actions are getting in the way. They suggest your lack of vision, belief, and faith restricts God from releasing His financial power and blessings into your life.

Their primary supposition is that you have to believe God has the power to change your life. Next, because you believe in God's power to change your life, your actions must show this because faith without works is dead. In order for God to unleash financial blessings into your life, you first have to accept and believe in God's math, which suggests the more you give, the more you receive, as illustrated when Jesus said: *"Give, and it will be given to you. A good measure, pressed down, shaken together and running over, will be poured into your lap. For with the measure you use, it will be measured to you."* (NIV, Luke 6:38). You will hear these preachers say "sow a seed" with a $50, $100, $500, and $1,000 contribution, and you will see God's favor in your life.

This is evident when you turn on the television and listen to one of these prosperity preachers. The last five minutes of the broadcast is spent trying to persuade you to make a donation. And if you give a donation, you will get – a better relationship with God, favor, financial blessings, forgiveness, healing; you name it.

But your giving cannot be sporadic. It must be consistent. In order to unlock the blessings, plans, and future God has for you, you must be faithful and consistent in your giving. Faithful means committing to a specified amount, and consistent means reoccurring on a fixed schedule. Their supposition is that systematic benevolence is best displayed by tithing, and that is why God designed it.

This is where the conspiracy, lies, and misrepresentations begin.

Why is it a conspiracy?

A conspiracy is an agreement by two or more persons conspired in secret to commit evil, fraudulent, unlawful, or other wrongful acts. Many prosperity preachers and church organizations have known for a long time that present-day tithing looks nothing like God's original design, and they don't care. Therefore, they have misrepresented and misquoted scripture in order to maintain a scheme that has fraudulently separated you from your money. This scheme is tithing.

The tithing scheme goes like this: if you receive any amount of monetary income, that income should be tithed. It does not matter whether you are a child running a lemonade stand or a retired person living on social security. I have heard preachers say that 10 percent of the money received during birthdays and Christmas as a gift belongs to God.

Prosperity preachers and false teachers know that it will be hard to convince people to give 10 percent of their earnings to a church when 100 percent is sometimes not enough to make ends meet. When the "sow a seed" appeal doesn't work, these preachers resort to attacking your conscience, emotions, and religious convictions in order to get the 10 percent they demand. They do this by applying the carrot and stick principle. If you cannot gently motivate a donkey to move by putting a carrot in front of its face, you can make it move by beating it. The most effective stick used is generally this scripture: *"Will a man rob God? Yet ye have robbed me. But ye say, Wherein have we robbed thee? In tithes and offerings. Ye are cursed with a curse: for ye have robbed me, even this whole nation"* (Malachi 3:8-9). This passage is heard from the bully pulpit each week and accuses Christians of robbing God. Even worse, it is used to suggest that if you don't pay your tithe, you will be cursed!

You cannot rob God of something he did not ask for. The only people that claim robbery are the prosperity preachers and false teachers when you don't pay your tithe. Because most people do not understand tithing, they are easily deceived and continue to support a scheme that takes money away from them by false pretenses. Trusting followers, believing in false teachings, are lining the pockets of corrupt pastors, funding bloated salaries and excessive budgets, all in the name of serving God.

Let's see a real-life example of how ill-gotten tithe proceeds are used. In June 2015, a very prominent pastor in Atlanta, Georgia, succeeded in convincing his church to purchase a $65 million Gulfstream G650 Jet. As the argument went, the jet was needed because it would make it easier for the pastor to conduct his ministry globally. Apparently, Delta Airlines, headquartered in Atlanta, does not have enough domestic and international flights each day to suit his busy schedule.

Why can executives working for fortune 500 companies fly commercial and a pastor need a private jet?

There is nowhere in the Bible where Jesus, his disciples, or any of the Old Testament prophets traveled using a first-class chariot. I'm not suggesting a pastor must always rent a car, take a bus, or fly on the cheapest airline to reach their destination, but a private plane is absolutely ridiculous!

Do you believe God is pleased with this level of excess when there are millions of people around the world who lack food, clean water, suitable clothing, and adequate housing?

The $65 million used to purchase that jet could have purchased a lot of groceries, kept families from being evicted and foreclosed, kept kids in school, and paid for needed medical treatment.

God's grace and blessings are free and you do not have to pay tithe to receive them. Let's be clear - *"God loveth a cheerful giver"* *(2 Corinthians 9:7)*. If you are a Christian, you should give money to whatever ministry you are loyal to. However, your financial support should not be called tithes. It is an offering. You will learn later in this book why it is inappropriate to call your offering tithes. Also, you will learn the Bible-based way to finance church organizations.

**Chapter Summary**

Religion is for sale, and there are many pastors, preachers, churches, and Christian denominations getting rich by selling you the idea that you must give God (them) 10 percent of your income in order to secure a financial blessing and obtain prosperity. If this does not work, they will resort to scare tactics and accuse you of robbing God, and the punishment for your sin may result in disfellowship from the church or a curse imposed on your ability to obtain wealth.

These prosperity preachers and false teachers knowingly misinterpret scripture in order to coerce you to give them 10 percent of your hard-earned money first, before you pay your bills, help your family, and provide for those in need. They maintain that the tithe you give should be predictable and consistent in order to sustain God's favor. They make no apology for the demands they put on your money and are not shy in how they use it, even when it is obvious that your tithe is being used to sustain their extravagant lifestyle – expensive trips, airplanes, cars, mansions, and wardrobe.

It is time for devout, well-intentioned, God-fearing believers to become more mature in their knowledge about tithing and stewardship: *"Then we will no longer be infants, tossed back and forth by the waves, and blown here and there by every wind of teaching and by the cunning and craftiness of people in their deceitful scheming" (NIV, Ephesians 4:14).*

# Chapter 2

# When Did Tithing Begin?

Before we learn when tithing began in the Bible, we should establish the literal definition of the tithe. The Hebrew definition of the word tithe is "a tenth" of something that is physical in nature. A tithe in present-day churches is no longer physical in nature but is based on a fiat currency. A fiat currency is a currency a government has declared to be legal tender but is not backed by a physical commodity.

Doesn't it seem strange that a man-made invention (fiat currency) is now regarded by tithing proponents as holy?

<u>The Tithe of Abraham</u>

Tithe first appeared in the Bible when Abraham gave tithes to Melchizedek: *"<u>And Melchizedek king of Salem brought forth bread and wine: and he was the priest of the most high God. And he blessed him, and said, Blessed be Abram of the most high God, possessor of heaven and earth: And blessed be the most high God, which hath delivered thine enemies into thy hand. And he gave him tithes of all</u>"* (Genesis 14:18-20). However, this tithe was different from the tithe required by Mosaic Law and the tithe currently collected in present-day churches. There are several differences between these three tithes that will be discussed in detail. <u>The tithe given to Melchizedek was not taken from Abraham's personal assets or wealth</u>. Unlike the Mosaic tithe, which is the portion taken from a person's flock and fields, the tithe that was given (not paid) to Melchizedek came from the spoils of war and plunder taken from conquered kings. This would have likely included cattle and livestock, gold, jewels, clothing, and such things that can be easily carried away. The Bible does not say Abraham was obligated to give a tenth of the spoils to Melchizedek. This transfer of wealth was <u>not</u> a precedent-setting occurrence, as some may think or would like to suggest. There was no command or law in the Bible that required Abraham to give a tithe to Melchizedek or any other priest. The tithe given to Melchizedek was a one-time freewill offering. Abraham had many servants and hundreds of livestock. At no point were any of these offered as a tithe. Unlike what we see in present-day churches, the tithe given to Melchizedek was not earned income, salary, or wages. It was plunder, the wealth and goods taken from defeated kings. Anyone insisting tithing was established by Abraham does not understand the biblical text or is purposely trying to mislead you.

The other biblical references where the spoils of war are given to priests show that the amount was far less than 10 percent or criticized altogether. There are two passages in scripture where this is illustrated.

The first occurs in Numbers chapter 31. After a successful war against the Midianites, Moses was given instructions by God on how to divide the plunder and spoils of war: _"And the children of Israel took the women of Midian captive, with their little ones, and took as spoil all their cattle, all their flocks, and all their goods... And they took all the spoil, and all the prey, both of men and of beasts...And the Lord spake unto Moses, saying, Take the sum of the prey that was taken, both of man and of beast, thou, and Eleazar the priest, and the chief fathers of the congregation: And divide the prey into two parts; between them that took the war upon them, who went out to battle, and between all the congregation: And levy a tribute unto the Lord of the men of war which went out to battle: one soul of five hundred, both of the persons, and of the beeves, and of the asses, and of the sheep: Take it of their half, and give it unto Eleazar the priest, for an heave offering of the Lord. And of the children of Israel's half, thou shalt take one portion of fifty, of the persons, of the beeves, of the asses, and of the flocks, of all manner of beasts, and give them unto the Levites, which keep the charge of the tabernacle of the Lords"_ (Numbers 31:9, 11, 25-30).

These verses show how the plunder and spoils were divided into two parts, between those that took part in the fighting and to the entire congregation. From the portion going to the men that fought in the battle, Moses commanded that $1/500^{th}$ or 0.2 percent of the plunder be given to Eleazer to be offered as a heave offering to the Lord. From the portion going to all the congregation, Moses commanded that $1/50^{th}$ or 2 percent be given to the Levites who take care of the tabernacle (I won't go into detail here, but please understand that all Levites were not priests like Moses and Aaron and had other duties).

The table below summarizes Numbers 31:32-42 and shows the actual number of sheep, cattle, donkeys, and virgins that were taken and given as tribute to the priests and Levites, with the remaining portion going to the rest of the congregation.

|  | Total Captured | Congregation Portion | Priest Portion (1/500th) | Levite Portion (1/50th) |
|---|---|---|---|---|
| Sheep | 337,500 | 330,075 | 6,750 | 675 |
| Cattle | 36,000 | 35,208 | 720 | 72 |
| Donkeys | 35,000 | 34,239 | 700 | 61 |
| Virgins | 16,000 | 15,648 | 320 | 32 |

The amount allocated to the priests and Levites was much less than 10 percent. Because the Israelites did not suffer any human casualties during the war, the officers and captains over the army decided to give more than what was commanded: *"And the officers which were over thousands of the host...said unto Moses, Thy servants have taken the sum of the men of war which are under our charge, and there lacketh not one man of us. We have therefore brought an oblation for the LORD, what every man hath gotten, of jewels of gold, chains, and bracelets, rings, earrings, and tablets, to make an atonement for our souls before the LORD. And Moses and Eleazar the priest took the gold of them, even all wrought jewels"* (Numbers 31:48-51).

The gold and jewels given to the priests were a freewill offering. It was not commanded or required by Moses. Moreover, the portion specified to go to the priests and Levites as tribute (see table above) did not become an established practice. This is supported in another Old Testament occurrence where reserving a portion of the plunder for the priests was later criticized.

In 1st Samuel we see what happens to the spoils of war: *"Now go and smite Amalek, and utterly destroy all that they have, and spare them not; but slay both man and woman, infant and suckling, ox and sheep, camel and ass…And Saul smote the Amalekites from Havilah until thou comest to Shur, that is over against Egypt. And he took Agag the king of the Amalekites alive, and utterly destroyed all the people with the edge of the sword. But Saul and the people spared Agag, and the best of the sheep, and of the oxen, and of the fatlings, and the lambs, and all that was good, and would not utterly destroy them: but every thing that was vile and refuse, that they destroyed utterly"* (1 Samuel 15:3, 7-9).

From these verses, you see Saul did not follow all of Samuel's instructions. Samuel's expectations of Saul were based on principles governing warfare after the Jews entered Canaan: *"But of the cities of these people, which the LORD thy God doth give thee for an inheritance, thou shalt save alive nothing that breatheth: But thou shalt utterly destroy them; namely, the Hittites, and the Amorites, the Canaanites, and the Perizzites, the Hivites, and the Jebusites; as the LORD thy God hath commanded thee: That they teach you not to do after all their abominations, which they have done unto their gods; so should ye sin against the LORD your God"* (Deuteronomy 20:16-18). Saul was supposed to kill everything living; this included all people, cattle, and livestock.

Samuel was greatly displeased by Saul's disobedience and spoke harshly to him. Saul tries to justify his actions and disobedience when he says: *"I have performed the commandment of the LORD. And Samuel said, What meaneth then this bleating of the sheep in mine ears, and the lowing of the oxen which I hear? And Saul said, They have brought them from the Amalekites: for the people spared the best of the sheep and of the oxen, to sacrifice unto the LORD thy God; and the rest we have utterly destroyed"* (1 Samuel 15:13-15). Saul's excuse for keeping the sheep and oxen alive is because they would be offered as a sacrifice to the Lord; however, unlike the instructions that were given to Moses in Numbers 31, Samuel was not ordered by God to give this command.

The Tithe of Jacob

A more cunning tithing advocate may try to use the oath that Jacob made while traveling to Haran as proof that tithing was established by Abraham and was followed by his decedents. First, let's establish the background for why Jacob was traveling to Haran, a city in a region called Padan Aram.

In Genesis chapters 27 and 28 - Jacob, with the help of his mother, Rebekah, succeeded in tricking his father, Isaac, into giving him the birthright. Esau, the eldest son and rightful receiver of the birthright, is angered by this treachery. Rebekah overhears that Esau plans to kill Jacob after their father is dead and devises a plan to have Jacob go to her brother's, Laban, home in Haran for a few days in order to give Esau time to cool down. Continuing with her deception, Rebekah tells Isaac that she is weary of the women in the surrounding land and that it would be pointless to continue living if Jacob were to marry one of them. Wanting to please his wife and being totally unaware of how he is being manipulated, Isaac tells Jacob to go to Padan Aram and marry one of his cousins.

While on the way to Haran, Jacob paused to sleep and had an incredible dream where God made himself known to him and promised that his descendants would span the entire earth and that He would look after him wherever he went. It was after this dream that Jacob made a vow to return a tenth of everything God gives him: *"And Jacob vowed a vow, saying, If God will be with me, and will keep me in this way that I go, and will give me bread to eat, and raiment to put on, So that I come again to my father's house in peace; then shall the LORD be my God: And this stone, which I have set for a pillar, shall be God's house: and of all that thou shalt give me I will surely give the tenth unto thee"* (Genesis 28:20-22).

These two verses are loaded with information. The key word in verse 20 is "if." The word "if" is the conjunction in this passage, implying that Jacob's later actions are predicated on some condition being met. Jacob says that **if** God will be with him, give him food and clothing so that he can come back to his father's house in peace, **then** the Lord will be his God. If God is faithful in doing these things that Jacob asks, then he will give God a tenth of his possessions. Prior to this experience, Jacob had not made a decision to make God the Lord of his life. Most importantly, his vow was conditional. Only when he is allowed to return home peacefully will the Lord be his God. Jacob attempts to bargain with God as if God is someone to be bargained with.

Anyone that uses this story as support that Jacob is carrying on the tithing tradition of his grandfather, Abraham, is misguided or purposely trying to mislead. This story does not present a credible argument or establish a sound basis for tithing. Once Jacob returned to Canaan, there is no record of him honoring his pledge to God by returning a tenth of his possessions. It appears that Jacob reneged on his promise.

**Tithe in the Wilderness**

A tithe is not mentioned again in the Bible until Moses, when tithing became a religious practice. Before the Israelites crossed into the Promised Land, God told Moses that the priests and Levites would not have a part of the land inheritance the other tribes would receive: _"The priests the Levites, and all the tribe of Levi, shall have no part nor inheritance with Israel: they shall eat the offerings of the LORD made by fire, and his inheritance. Therefore shall they have no inheritance among their brethren: the LORD is their inheritance, as he hath said unto them"_ (Deuteronomy 18:1-2). Their inheritance was God and the priesthood. Aaron, his sons, and their male descendants would serve as priests and be assigned work related to the sanctuary: _"And the LORD said unto Aaron, Thou and thy sons and thy father's house with thee shall bear the iniquity of the sanctuary: and thou and thy sons with thee shall bear the iniquity of your priesthood...And ye shall keep the charge of the sanctuary, and the charge of the altar...Therefore thou and thy sons with thee shall keep your priest's office for everything of the altar, and within the vail; and ye shall serve: I have given your priest's office unto you as a service of gift: and the stranger that cometh nigh shall be put to death"_ (Numbers 18:1, 5, 7). The other Levites were to have other professions and support Aaron and his sons by attending to the needs of the tabernacle, whatever was needed: _"And thy brethren also of the tribe of Levi, the tribe of thy father, bring thou with thee, that they may be joined unto thee, and minister unto thee...And they shall keep thy charge, and the charge of all the tabernacle: only they shall not come nigh the vessels of the sanctuary and the altar, that neither they, nor ye also, die. And they shall be joined unto thee, and_ *keep the charge of the tabernacle of the congregation, for all the service of the tabernacle: and a stranger shall not come nigh unto you" (Numbers 18:2-4).* This required the Levites to be skilled in a variety of trades.

Non-Levites were not allowed to be priests or participate in any work related to the sanctuary. Their role was to support the priests and the Levites by giving them 10 percent of everything grown from the land so they would not have to grow their own food and could dedicate their time to looking after the sanctuary.

The Israelites were instructed to give 10 percent (tithe) of the crops grown and the tenth animal from the herd that passed under the rod to the Lord as these were considered holy: *"And all the tithe of the land, whether of the seed of the land, or of the fruit of the tree, is the LORD's: it is holy unto the LORD… And concerning the tithe of the herd, or of the flock, even of whatsoever passeth under the rod, the tenth shall be holy unto the LORD" (Leviticus 27:30, 32).* These provisions were provided so that the priests and Levites had food during the time they were engaged in the work of the temple. Because the Levites were not given an inheritance, the Israelites also had to give them cities to dwell in and common land outside the city for their cattle, goods, and animals: *"Command the children of Israel, that they give unto the Levites of the inheritance of their possession cities to dwell in; and ye shall give also unto the Levites suburbs for the cities round about them. And the cities shall they have to dwell in; and the suburbs of them shall be for their cattle, and for their goods, and for all their beasts" (Numbers 35:2-3).*

This tithing practice was carried on for many generations. The tithe was not collected during the Babylonian captivity, but resumed when the Jews were allowed to return to their homeland and rebuild the temple: *"Thus saith Cyrus king of Persia, the Lord God of heaven…hath charged me to build him a house at Jerusalem, which is in Judah. Who is there among you of all his people?…let him go up to Jerusalem…and build the house of the Lord God of Israel, which is in Jerusalem" (Ezra 1:2-3),* and *"The priest the son of Aaron shall be with the Levites, when the Levites take tithes: and the Levites shall bring up the tithe of the tithes unto the house of our God, to the chambers, into the treasure house. For the children of Israel and the children of Levi shall bring the offering of the corn, of the new wine, and the oil, unto the chambers, where are the vessels of the sanctuary, and the priests that minister, and the porters, and the singers: and we will not forsake the house of our God"* (Nehemiah 10:38-39).

Tithing in the wilderness was a work-in-progress that did not reach its final state until the Israelites reached Canaan, their final destination. Moses developed the tithing doctrine over the forty years the Jews wandered in the desert, and it was not until the close of Deuteronomy, the last month of the fortieth year – before he died, that Moses gave them his final instructions. Since the Jews would no longer be wanderers and would be entering a more civilized existence, the laws given on Mount Sinai needed adjustment to account for their change in environment. The first eleven chapters of Deuteronomy summarize Moses' instructions and the adjustments that were made. This included the tithing law.

During the forty years the Jews wandered in the wilderness, the manner in which the Israelites performed their tithing obligation was largely unregulated. Because their environment and existence were about to change, new instructions and administration practices were needed. Moses decided to make a change to how the tithe was distributed. Moses said: *"Ye shall not do after all the things that we do here [within the wilderness] this day, every man whatsoever is right in his own eyes"* (Deuteronomy 12:8). While they were in the wilderness, most Israelites lived near the tabernacle, and it was easy for them to deposit the tithe in the temple treasury. However, the Land of Canaan was a large territory that expanded an area of 15,000 miles making it more difficult for the Israelites tribes living in the forty-eight cities scattered across the territory to bring the tithe to a central location. Acknowledging the burden the wilderness setup would create if it were not changed, Moses authorized forty-eight cities as official sites where tithes could be collected and stored in the designated tithing years: *"So all the cities which ye shall give to the Levites shall be forty and eight cities: them ye shall give with their suburbs"* (Numbers 35:7).

In Canaan, religious activities would become more regulated and precise. Moses told the Israelites: *"there shall be a place which the LORD your God shall choose to cause his name to dwell there; thither shall ye bring all that I command you; your burnt offerings, and your sacrifices, your tithes, and the heave offering of your hand, and all your choice vows which ye vow unto the LORD" (Deuteronomy 12:11)*. In addition to all these items brought to the priests, Deuteronomy 12:6 also includes: *"the firstlings of your herds and flocks."* It should be noted that the law of the firstlings (firstborn of the herds and flocks and the first of the fruit of the harvest from farms) is a very different set of laws than those of tithing. It is very important that they are not confused or misinterpreted as is often done by preachers who want to be the first paid, so they inappropriately apply the word "first" to include your income. The law of firstlings is not for present-day Christians and was never intended to be. For further study on firstlings see Numbers 3:12-13, 40-45; 8:16-18, and for first fruits, see Leviticus 23:10-14.

While the Israelites were wandering through the wilderness, they were allowed to give the Levites the tithe and first fruits in any manner they wanted. The proof statement for this is when Moses said: *"Ye shall not do after all the things that we do here this day, every man whatsoever is right in his own eyes" (Deuteronomy 12:8)*. Once they crossed into Canaan, they were expected to operate under a stricter set of laws, and this included tithing. As you will see, the tithing practices of the Israelites in Canaan are very different from the tithing practiced by present-day Christians.

**Tithing in Canaan**

There were economic reasons for why the tithing system adopted in the wilderness required change. Moses wanted to establish an equitable system that would not give a tribe an unfair advantage. Therefore, Moses devised a very equitable system, one that prevented the priests and Levites from living in poverty or wealth.

The nomadic forty-year period in the wilderness impeded substantial increases in agricultural production and livestock. As such, Moses probably did not think it was important to fully address the law of tithing in the wilderness. Once the Israelites crossed into Canaan, things would be different. The eleven tribes would receive their land inheritance and would no longer have to wander as nomads. This would allow them the opportunity to really embrace an agrarian lifestyle as farmers and herdsmen. Naturally, as the amount of food and livestock produced each year increased, the amount apportioned to the Levites would grow larger. Moses recognized that a great deal of livestock and produce would be arriving at the central sanctuary each year for the Levite's benefit. Moses realized that eleven tribes, each tithing 10 percent of all crops and livestock every year in perpetuity, would eventually give the Levites a considerable financial advantage over the other tribes. This could not be allowed.

Moses devised a plan that would equalize the situation for all Israelites to have a share in the blessings provided by God. Moses commanded that the eleven tribes set aside 10 percent of their harvest and livestock production each year. He then commanded the tithe be brought to the chosen place for where the temple would be. To accomplish this in a pragmatic way, Moses changed the law by allowing the tithe to be converted into money without adding the penalty of a fifth (twenty percent) extra: *"But if he will at all redeem it, then he shall add a fifth part thereof unto thy estimation" (Leviticus 27:13)*. The Law had previously prohibited the Israelites from giving the priests and Levites a tithing substitute such as gold, jewelry, or money. The tithe had always been crops produced from the land and cattle. This new provision allowed the Israelites that lived a long way from the temple to exchange the tithe for money, travel to the place the Lord had chosen, and spend the money to purchase anything they desired to eat or drink: *"If the way be too long for thee, so that thou art not able to carry it; or if the place be too far from thee... Then shalt thou turn it into money, and bind up the money in thine hand... And thou shalt bestow that money for whatsoever thy soul lusteth after, for oxen, or for sheep, or for wine, or for strong drink, or for whatsoever thy soul desireth: and thou shalt eat there before the LORD thy God... And the Levite that is within thy gates; thou shalt not forsake him; for he hath no part nor inheritance with thee" (Deuteronomy 14:24-27)*.

Did you see that?

Once they arrived at the designated location, they were allowed to spend the money however they pleased because it was considered a festive occasion. However, the Israelites were instructed not to forsake the Levites and were required to share their purchase of food and drink with them. This provision prevented the Jews from circumventing the rule that required them to give their crops, sheep, and cattle to the priests by claiming that the trip was too long and burdensome. Israelites that lived near the temple were still expected to bring their tithe of grain, oil, and livestock to the sanctuary.

This was a very equitable arrangement. In the third and sixth year of a seven-year sabbatical period, the Levites were able to receive the full tithe (minus the portion designated for the strangers, widows, and orphans living among them). This would prevent the Levites from overly benefiting from the tithe brought to them each year while others lacked adequate food.

The final tithing law looked like this: the Israelites were allowed to share the tithe with the Levites during the festival seasons each year, and every third and sixth year, the Levites would receive the full tithe for their personal consumption but had to share it with the poor.

It should be fully understood that there was only one tithing plan devised by Moses and the tithe held back for the poor was not a "second" or "third" tithe. To find any reference to a "second" or "third" tithe one has to look outside the Bible for various Jewish interpretations. This is a slippery slope that cannot be trusted. Churches that teach a "second" and "third" tithe are teaching a false doctrine.

**Tithe: Part of the Social Safety Net**

Every third year the Law required the Israelites to refrain from delivering the tithe of their harvest (not flocks and herds) to the priests at the central temple. The tithe would stay in the forty-eight cities and be eaten by the Levites, the non-Israelites living among them, the fatherless and widows in order to keep them from going hungry: *"At the end of three years thou shalt bring forth all the tithe of thine increase the same year, and shalt lay it up within thy gates: And the Levite, (because he hath no part nor inheritance with thee,) and the stranger, and the fatherless, and the widow, which are within thy gates, shall come, and shall eat and be satisfied; that the LORD thy God may bless thee in all the work of thine hand which thou doest"* (Deuteronomy 14:28-29). If the Israelites faithfully fed the poor, God promised to continue blessing them. It was God's plan that no one in the community should go hungry and need to steal in order to eat. In the third and sixth year, the tithe would be used as part of their general welfare program. The general welfare program allowed the poor to eat from the portions of the field that were not gleaned by the reapers: *"When ye reap the harvest of your land, thou shalt not wholly reap the corners of thy field, neither shalt thou gather the gleanings of thy harvest. And thou shalt not glean thy vineyard, neither shalt thou gather every grape of thy vineyard; thou shalt leave them for the poor and stranger"* (Leviticus 19:9-10). This was so important it was also stated in Leviticus 23:22 and Deuteronomy 24:21.

We see this practice carried out in the book of Ruth. Ruth supported herself and her Mother-in-Law, Naomi, by gleaning Boaz's fields: *"Let me now go to the field, and glean ears of corn after him in whose sight I shall find grace...And she went, and came, and gleaned in the field after the reapers: and her hap was to light on a part of the field belonging unto Boaz"* (Ruth 2:2-3).

Even in wealthy countries like the United States, there are people that experience hunger every day. There are millions of children missing meals or eating low-quality food because their parents are unable to feed them. In many cases, the free or reduced lunch program in the school cafeteria is the only access these children have to food, and holidays and the summer break from school are especially difficult to endure.

Can you imagine how many people would be blessed if local churches established a social safety net that distributed food to the poor?

The tithing system God told Moses to implement ensured an equitable distribution of food for priests, Levites, and the poor. Now that system has morphed into a mechanism to fund the purchase of expensive church buildings, $65 million dollar airplanes, and an avenue to maintain the opulence of pastors who feel they are entitled to a lifestyle that vastly exceeds the average member in the congregation. God's equitable and holy tithing system has been perverted and debased into something that is totally unrecognizable from its original form and intent.

**Tithing: Not Required by All**

Most people are not aware of this but not all non-Levites tithed. Only farmers and herdsmen were required to tithe. Since not all Levites were priests, it should not seem strange that not all non-Levites were farmers and herdsmen. In order for society to advance, thrive, and flourish, the distribution of labor is needed. Progress is restricted if there is no division of labor. Moreover, it is impractical for everyone to do the same thing. Expertise, craftsmen, and trades will not be developed. We are not blessed to have the same talents and abilities. Some are better equipped to be doctors, judges, teachers, engineers, soldiers, etc. Therefore, it did not make sense for every non-Levite living in Canaan to be a farmer or herdsmen.

**Chapter Summary**

The tithe Abraham gave Melchizedek was plunder. It was a nonrecurring offering, and there was nothing holy about it. There were no instructions for what it should include. Therefore, it is foolish to use Abraham as the progenitor of tithing. The same rationale can be applied to Jacob. The Bible provides no evidence that Jacob upheld his promise.

While the Israelites were wandering in the wilderness, tithing was largely unregulated. When the Israelites reached Canaan, it became necessary for tithing practices to be more regulated with established rules and governance. Moses created an equitable tithing system that ensured the Levites did not overly benefit while the other tribes, including widows, orphans, and the poor, lived without food. The Israelites were allowed to use the tithe for their personal consumption as well as share it with the Levites and the poor. The tithe withheld for the poor in the third and sixth year was not considered a "second" and "third" tithe. It was the same tithe.

The fact the Israelites were allowed to use and share the tithe with their surrounding community seems strange when we contrast this with the way tithe is used today. Because of sincere ignorance or greed, many preachers, evangelists, and church denominations have departed from the biblical foundation of the scriptures that clearly shows a sharing of the tithe. They misapply the law of firstlings and first fruits in an effort to claim the first tenth of all income, even though scripture is clear that it was the tenth animal that passed under the rod that was tithed, not the first. Prosperity preachers and false teachers have seized this opportunity from such widespread ignorance. They feel entitled to 10 percent of the money that each Christian (including children) earns and have no intention of sharing it with you or anyone else. They even send demand letters threatening to disfellowship you if the full tithe is not received. It is past time for God's people to wake up, get educated, and stop being duped by false doctrines and return to the Holy Scriptures for direction.

## Chapter 3

## Who Has the Right To Receive Tithe?

The Bible clearly states that only descendants from the tribe of Levi are authorized to receive and live off the tithe: _"That we should bring the firstfruits of our dough, and our offerings, and the fruit of all manner of trees, of wine and of oil, unto the priests, to the chambers of the house of our God; and the tithes of our ground unto the Levites, that the same Levites might have the tithes in all the cities of our tillage. And the priest the son of Aaron shall be with the Levites, when the Levites take tithes: and the Levites shall bring up the tithe of the tithes unto the house of our God, to the chambers, into the treasure house"_ _(Nehemiah 10:37-38)_. This fact was well understood by the Jews. Present-day Christians believe that this law, along with many other Mosaic laws, was abolished. Paul's writings reflect that many ordinances were abolished after Christ's death: _"Blotting out the handwriting of ordinances that was against us, which was contrary to us, and took it out of the way, nailing it to the cross"_ _(Colossians 2:14)_; however, not one word of Paul's writings suggests that a non-Jew or a non-Levite has the right to receive tithes. On the contrary, Paul's writings and actions show the opposite.

Before I go any further, let me remind you that Jesus and his disciples were not priests or Levites. Therefore, no matter how often they visited the synagogue, they could not receive and eat from the tithes. Jesus was from the tribe of Judah and was a carpenter before he began his ministry: _"Is not this the carpenter"_ _(Mark 6:3)_. Once Jesus began his ministry he was recognized as a teacher or rabbi: _"When the Pharisees saw this, they said to his disciples, "Why does your teacher eat with tax collectors and sinners?"_ _(NRSV, Matthew 9:11)_ and _"Then Peter said to Jesus, "Rabbi, it is good for us to be here"_ _(NRSV, Mark 9:5)_. Four of Jesus' disciples – Peter, Andrew, James, and John were fishermen: _"And Jesus, walking by the sea of Galilee, saw two brethren, Simon called Peter, and Andrew his brother, casting a net into the sea: for they were fishers…And going on from thence, he saw other two brethren, James the_ *son of Zebedee, and John his brother, in a ship with Zebedee their father, mending their nets"* (Matthew 4:18, 21). Although Jesus spent a lot of time reading and teaching in the temple: *"As his custom was, he went into the synagogue on the sabbath day, and stood up for to read"* (Luke 4:16), he and his disciples had to find and buy their own food: *"Jesus went on the sabbath day through the corn; and his disciples were an hungered, and began to pluck the ears of corn and to eat"* (Matthew 12:1) and *"For his disciples were gone away unto the city to buy meat"* (John 4:8).

Even after Jesus' death and resurrection, there is no biblical record that the disciples were instructed or allowed to receive tithe. On the contrary, the disciples and early Christians were persecuted by the Jewish assembly and had to be responsible for their own financial support. Paul took great pride in working to keep from being a burden to others: *"Surely you remember, brothers and sisters, our toil and hardship; we worked night and day in order not to be a burden to anyone while we preached the gospel of God to you"* (NIV, 1 Thessalonians 2:9) and *"Nor did we eat anyone's food without paying for it. On the contrary, we worked night and day, laboring and toiling so that we would not be a burden to any of you"* (NIV, 2 Thessalonians 3:8). Anything that Paul could not supply from his own labor he received as gifts.

The fact that Paul and none of the other New Testament writers wrote anything about receiving a tenth of someone's income is noteworthy. The period after Christ's death was the perfect time to establish new rules, laws, and governance practices because the Christian church was in its infancy. All converts were new Christians. Many of the converts were Jews and already familiar with the tithing system. No one doubts the disciples and other evangelists needed funds in order to spread the gospel across the world.

So why didn't the disciples and New Testament writers say anything about tithing?

Because they understood the Jewish tithing system prohibited anyone other than priests and Levites from receiving tithe. They understood the tithe of the land and herd are holy to the Lord, and everything else that is given is an offering.

Tithing supporters will argue that Paul and the disciples continued the tithing system and will misquote the few scriptures in the New Testament that discuss collections. The most notable scripture used to support tithing is: *"Regarding the relief offering for poor Christians that is being collected, you get the same instructions I gave the churches in Galatia. Every Sunday each of you make an offering and put it in safekeeping. Be as generous as you can. When I get there you'll have it ready, and I won't have to make a special appeal"* (MSG, 1 Corinthians 16:1-3). Somehow, they have turned weekly collections for the poor into tithing.

Paul is requesting for money to be put aside each Sunday so the funds will be available before he arrives. Each member should put something aside for the poor each week; not for him and the other disciples. Notice what Paul is saying. Paul did not tell the Corinthians to set aside 10 percent of their income. Paul also wasn't talking about grain and cattle. Paul was requesting the relief offering collection for the poor be orderly, not haphazard as evident in some church services. An orderly collection is a continuance of prior counsel he gave about order in church meetings: *"Let all things be done decently and in order"* (1 Corinthians 14:40). Paul probably wanted to separate church services from money-raising events so that the focus could remain on worship and teaching. Some of you may attend church services where appeals are made to financially support a special cause. The service is usually disrupted until the target amount of money is raised. Instead of singing, praying, and bible study, the worship service looks more like a fundraiser.

Another scripture often used to defend tithing is: *"The elders who direct the affairs of the church well are worthy of double honor, especially those whose work is preaching and teaching. For Scripture says, "Do not muzzle an ox while it is treading out the grain," and "The worker deserves his wages"* (NIV, 1 Timothy 5:17-18). Although Paul did not receive payment for his work in the ministry, he acknowledged that people who work hard at preaching and teaching should receive payment for their work. But Paul never said that he or anyone else should be paid from the tithes.

Hundreds of thousands of people became Christians during the early church without a 10 percent tithe, and the message of Jesus Christ still spread throughout Europe and Asia. In Chapter 6, we will look at the Old and New Testament model used to support church operations.

**Chapter Summary**

Pastors, ministers, and church organizations that insist on collecting tithe from their members and use the Bible to legitimize this practice are outside the will of God. Only Levites and the priests had the right and authority to receive tithe. The Laws governing tithing were not changed after Christ's death. Paul and the disciples understood that they did not have the authority, nor were they directed by Jesus, to make changes to the tithing system put in place by Moses.

It is totally acceptable for those that commit themselves to laboring for the ministry be paid for their work. However, it is unacceptable for their payment to come from earnings collected as a tithe. The tithe was regarded as holy, was governed by very specific guidelines, and included crops and livestock. Payment or financial support provided to ministers, pastors, church conferences, and religious organizations should be considered gifts. In giving, there is no specified amount required. The heart and motive for your giving are what matters most.

# Chapter 4

## Who Was Really Cursed in Malachi 3:9?

Every weekend in churches all over the world, church leaders proclaim that a robbery is taking place, that Christians are robbing God by withholding the tithe: *"Will a man rob God? Yet ye have robbed me. But ye say, Wherein have we robbed thee? In tithes and offerings. Ye are cursed with a curse: for ye have robbed me, even this whole nation" (Malachi 3:8-9)*. This is probably the most misrepresented tithing scripture in the Bible. This passage is read from the pulpit and recited by the congregation as proof that Christians are robbing God every time they neglect to pay their tithe. Sadly, there are millions of people who believe this lie and they are the ones that are truly getting robbed each week.

Why is it so easy to misrepresent this scripture and fool millions of people?

Probably because they have not read Malachi chapters 1 and 2.

If you read the first and second chapters of Malachi, you will recognize that Malachi's message is directed at the priests. Malachi accuses the priests of offering as sacrifice polluted bread, blind, lame, and sick animals on the alter: *"Ye offer polluted bread upon mine altar; and ye say, Wherein have we polluted thee? In that ye say, The table of the LORD is contemptible. And if ye offer the blind for sacrifice, is it not evil? and if ye offer the lame and sick, is it not evil? Offer it now unto thy governor; will he be pleased with thee, or accept thy person? saith the LORD of hosts" (Malachi 1:6-8)*. He asks them a rhetorical question, whether they think offering blind, lame, and sick animals is an evil practice, and would their governor be pleased if they presented him with a similar offering. You can hear the disgust in his voice. Malachi is outraged that the priests are taking liberties with God that they wouldn't dare take with a man. They do not seem to care that their offering is not accepted: *"I have no pleasure in you, saith the LORD of hosts, neither will I accept an offering at your hand" (Malachi 1:10)*. The priests are merely going through the motions and are offering profane sacrifices because pleasing God has become wearisome to them: *"Ye said also, Behold, what a weariness is it!" (Malachi 1:13).*

How do I know that Malachi is speaking specifically to the priests and not the Israelite congregation?

He said so: *"O priests, that despise my name" (Malachi 1:6)* and *"O ye priests, this commandment is for you" (Malachi 2:1).* He further tells the priests that if they will not hear and apply his commands to their heart they will be cursed: *"If ye will not hear, and if ye will not lay it to heart, to give glory unto my name, saith the LORD of hosts, I will even send a curse upon you, and I will curse your blessings: yea, I have cursed them already, because ye do not lay it to heart" (Malachi 2:2).* He follows up his address to them by saying: *"And ye shall know that I have sent this command unto you, that my covenant will be with Levi, saith the Lord of hosts" (Malachi 2:4).* In the Bible, a covenant is an agreement between God and his people, in which God makes a promise to his people and usually expects certain conduct in return.

As you can see in the preceding paragraph, Malachi is speaking to the priest; those from the tribe of Levi! He is not speaking to the congregation. We learned in Chapter 3 that only Aaron's descendants were allowed to serve as priests, and Aaron was a Levite.

These priests had gone astray, abused their position, and caused others to break God's law even though they were the ones trusted to be God's messengers: *"For the priest's lips should keep knowledge, and they should seek the law at his mouth: for he is the messenger of the LORD of hosts. But ye are departed out of the way; ye have caused many to stumble at the law; ye have corrupted the covenant of Levi, saith the LORD of hosts. Therefore have I also made you contemptible and base before all the people, according as ye have not kept my ways, but have been partial in the law" (Malachi 2:7-9).* Their behavior was outrageous. They stopped following God's ordinances just like their fathers before them, and now they were robbing God.

Exactly how were they robbing God?

The priests were withholding the best portions of the tithe and heave offerings brought to them by the Israelites for themselves and were sacrificing in its place blind, lame, and sick livestock, animals that were clearly unfit. It was very important that sheep, goats, and bulls offered as a sacrifice not have any blemishes: *"Ye shall offer at your own will a male without blemish, of the beeves, of the sheep, or of the goats. But whatsoever hath a blemish, that shall ye not offer: for it shall not be acceptable for you" (Leviticus 22:19-20)*. The term "without blemish" as it pertains to animal sacrifices occurs twice in Exodus, seventeen times in Leviticus, and seventeen times in Numbers, for a total of thirty-six times. Blemish, as defined in the Easton's Bible Dictionary, refers to an imperfection or bodily deformity excluding men from the priesthood (see Leviticus 21:17-23), and rendering animals unfit to be offered in sacrifice. In chapters 1 and 2 of Malachi, the prophet is talking about blemished animals.

Malachi 3:9 says: *"Ye are cursed with a curse: for ye have robbed me, even this whole nation."* Notice that the Bible doesn't say the whole nation is cursed even though everyone is robbing God. Malachi says the priests are cursed. Although the entire Jewish nation was robbing God, the priests were responsible for making sure the Jews followed God's ordinances. Instead, the priests were blind guides leading the blind, and they caused the whole Jewish nation to sin.

The pastors that preach tithing are misrepresenting scripture to convince you that anyone that does not pay tithe is robbing God when they are the ones committing a crime. It is really these prosperity preachers and false teachers that will find themselves cursed. They are blind guides leading you astray. They misrepresent scripture to their own advantage and use the money you give them for their own use. Their contempt is very similar to the evil perpetrated by Eli's sons when they misused the people's sacrifice: *"Now the sons of Eli were sons of Belial; they knew not the LORD. And the priest's custom with the people was, that, when any man offered sacrifice, the priest's servant came, while the flesh was in seething, with a fleshhook of three teeth in his hand; And he struck it into the pan, or kettle, or caldron, or pot; all that the fleshhook brought up the priest took for himself. So they did in Shiloh unto all the Israelites that came thither. Also before they burnt the fat, the priest's servant came, and said to the man that sacrificed, Give flesh to roast for the priest; for he will not have sodden flesh of thee, but raw. And if any man said unto him, Let them not fail to burn the fat presently, and then take as much as thy soul desireth; then he would answer him, Nay; but thou shalt give it me now: and if not, I will take it by force. Wherefore the sin of the young men was very great before the LORD: for men abhorred the offering of the LORD"* (1 Samuel 2:12-17).

First, as we learned in Chapter 3, only priests from the tribe of Levi have the right to receive tithe. Secondly, the Jews were not bringing money to the storehouse - they were bringing food. Most churches do not have a food pantry. Churches do not even store the money collected each week in a vault for very long – it is deposited in a bank. Banks are businesses that make money by charging interest on loans.

Have banks become the present-day storehouse?

Where is the social safety net in today's tithing system that allows patrons to partake of the tithe while sharing it with clergy and the poor?

It is outrageous how tithing advocates have taken parts of a Jewish practice and turned it into something that resembles nothing that Moses established.

**Chapter Summary**

Malachi 3:8-9 is probably the most misrepresented scripture tithing advocates quote in the Bible. They contend that anyone that does not pay tithe is robbing God and will be cursed. However, Malachi was not speaking to the Jewish nation, he was speaking to the priests. The priests were the ones criticized for robbing God and received the curse for failing to follow God's ordinances. They were withholding the best meats for themselves and offering God "blemished" sacrifices.

Pastors that knowingly deceive others by preaching a false tithing doctrine are the real thieves and are no different than the priests that Malachi rebuked. They are blind guides that lead God's people astray.

They have cherry picked certain principles from God's tithing system and turned it into something that looks nothing like Moses' design. It is an inequitable system that does not provide for the poor and allow prosperity preachers and false teachers to profit far beyond the members of their congregation.

## Chapter 5

## Why Should You Continue Giving?

Now that we have seen that it is unlawful for non-Levites to receive tithe and the early Christian church was not financially supported by the tithe, the question we need to answer is, should Christians continue supporting church organizations with their money?

Absolutely!

There are several scriptures, and stories in the Bible that prove giving is righteous, morally right, and has many financial and non-financial rewards. As we will see, some of the rewards can be life-saving.

**Charity is a sign of righteousness**

The first thing God requires is obedience. The Ten Commandments are a guide for what God requires from us and how He expects us to live. They are commandments because God expects us to comply with these ten simple rules, not out of fear but out of love: *"If ye love me, keep my commandments" (John 14:15)*. Love is the central theme of the commandments, and there is no greater commandment than this: *"Thou shalt love the Lord thy God with all thy heart, and with all thy soul, and with all thy mind, and with all thy strength: this is the first commandment. And the second is like, namely this, Thou shalt love thy neighbor as thyself. There is none other commandment greater than these" (Mark 12:30-31)*. The first and second commandments are not mutually exclusive.

You cannot consider yourself obedient to God, righteous, and a loving person if you neglect those in need. The Apostle John states this clearly: *"If anyone has material possessions and sees a brother or a sister in need but has no pity on them, how can the love of God be in that person?" (NIV, 1 John 3:17)*. The level and manner in which you give are directly correlated with your love for God and others. Jesus said: *"For where your treasure is, there your heart will be also" (Matthew 6:21)*. Our money tends to flow into things that are important to us. If you love God and serving him is important to you, a portion of your salary or wealth will be dedicated to aiding the needy or supporting organizations that are responsible for helping others. You should give responsibly and ensure that whatever organization you financially support is practicing good stewardship and is using the money to help the people it was intended for.

**Giving is a measure of your faith**

Many people make an excuse (what they really believe is a reason) for why they cannot give a portion of their money to a religious or charitable organization. You may have heard or even said yourself, "I don't have that much to give" or "I barely make enough to pay my bills." This may be true; however, the amount you have available to give is not as important as the attitude in which you give. *"Better is a little with righteousness, than vast revenues without justice" (NKJV, Proverbs 16:8)*. If all you have at the end of the month is two dollars, you should not feel ashamed about putting that in the offering plate or sending it to a charitable organization. No matter how poor you think you are, your two dollars is much more than what some people have.

While visiting the temple one day, Jesus told his disciples that a poor widow's offering of two mites was worth more than all the rich people's offering: *"Jesus sat down near the collection box in the Temple and watched as the crowds dropped in their money. Many rich people put in large amounts. Then a poor widow came and dropped in two small coins. Jesus called his disciples to him and said, "I tell you the truth, this poor widow has given more than all the others who are making contributions. For they gave a tiny part of their surplus, but she, poor as she is, has given everything she had to live on" (NLT, Mark 12:41-44)*. The Bible says that this poor widow gave all the money she had but notice that it does not say that she went hungry. The righteous know and understand that God will not forsake charitable people. They may not have great wealth, but their basic needs will always be provided. David revealed this truth when he said: *"I have been young, and now am old; yet I have not seen the righteous forsaken, nor his descendants begging bread"* (NKJV, Psalms 37:25).

Trust God. Give generously and often. Always remember: *"You must each decide in your heart how much to give. And don't give reluctantly or in response to pressure. "For God loves a person who gives cheerfully"* (NLT, 2 Corinthians 9:7) and "*the righteous are generous and keep giving"* (NRSV, Psalm 37:21).

Do you trust God to provide for your basic needs?

You should.

Paul was certain his needs would be provided when he said: *"You can be sure that God will take care of everything you need, his generosity exceeding even yours in the glory that pours out from Jesus"* (MSG, Philippians 4:19). There are several examples throughout the Bible that reveal that you can't beat God's giving. All you have to do is trust him.

Let's look at one example.

In 1 Kings verse 17 is a woman that had awesome faith, despite her poverty, and was willing to make Elijah a meal even though she was down to her last handful of meal and oil: *"And the word of the LORD came unto him, saying, Arise, get thee to Zarephath, which belongeth to Zidon, and dwell there: behold, I have commanded a widow woman there to sustain thee. So he arose and went to Zarephath. And when he came to the gate of the city, behold, the widow woman was there gathering of sticks: and he called to her, and said, Fetch me, I pray thee, a little water in a vessel, that I may drink. And as she was going to fetch it, he called to her, and said, Bring me, I pray thee, a morsel of bread in thine hand. And she said, As the LORD thy God liveth, I have not a cake, but an handful of meal in a barrel, and a little oil in a cruse: and, behold, I am gathering two sticks, that I may go in and dress it for me and my son, that we may eat it, and die. And Elijah said unto her, Fear not; go and do as thou hast said: but make me thereof a little cake first, and bring it unto me, and after make for thee and for thy son. For thus saith the LORD God of Israel, The barrel of meal shall not waste, neither shall the cruse of oil fail, until the day that the LORD sendeth rain upon the earth. And she went and did according to the saying of Elijah: and she, and he, and her house, did eat many days. And the barrel of meal wasted not, neither did the cruse of oil fail, according to the word of the LORD, which he spake by Elijah"* (1 Kings 17:8-16).

Can you imagine preparing to cook your last meal when you get a strange knock at your door, and the man standing there asks you to cook what little food you have left but feed him first?

That is what this woman did. Not only did she share her food with Elijah, she fed him first even though she doubted there was enough available to feed herself and her son! In fact, she believed this was her last meal, and afterward, she and her son would die from starvation.

But this woman and her son did not die! She trusted in God, put someone else's needs ahead of her own, and God blessed her so that she was able to make bread until the drought ended. Because of her faith and generosity, the blessings she received extended beyond having enough food. Later in the chapter, her son becomes sick and dies and is raised from the dead by Elijah. If not for this woman's faith, kindness, and willingness to give food to a man she had never met, she and her son would have likely starved to death. Even if they had found some way to escape starvation, if she had not fed Elijah, he may not have been around to resurrect her son. God rewards those that have faith in him, are charitable, and are willing to share with others.

**With Giving Comes More Blessings**

For those of you that already donate 10 percent of your income, perhaps you have the ability to do more. There are many ways to be charitable. Let's look at an example where a wealthy woman found a creative way to support a holy man of God. The passage is relatively long, so allow me to summarize it for you.

## The Shunamite Woman

In 2 Kings 4:8-37, a woman goes out of her way to be considerate. The Bible tells us that she was a wealthy woman, so it was not a sacrifice for her to share her food as we saw in the previous story. But she didn't just stop with sharing food; she made a comfortable room for Elisha so that whenever he passed by, he would have a place to rest after enjoying a meal. Now that's hospitality.

Elisha is so grateful for her hospitality that he tells his servant to ask her if there is anything that he can do for her to show his gratitude. She has everything she needs, except she does not have children. Elisha blesses her by promising that in nine months, she and her husband will have a son. Several years after her son is born, the child goes to visit his father in the field and severely injures his head. The child returns home to his mother, and tragically dies. The mother, devastated and upset that she has lost her only child, seeks Elisha for help. Elisha agrees to come to the woman's home and sees that the child has died. After praying to God, Elisha is able to restore the child's life.

By showing hospitality and being generous to a holy man of God, the Shunamite woman was rewarded with a son. She did not ask the prophet for a son, but she was blessed with one anyway. God knows our heart's desire. David said: _"Delight thyself also in the Lord: and he shall give thee the desires of thine heart"_ *(Psalm 37:4)*. There is no better way to ensure God's blessing and favor over your life than to do good to others.

The blessings for this woman and her family did not end there. In 2 Kings 8:1-6, Elisha helps this woman and her family avoid a seven-year famine. It is doubtful this woman would have ever had a son and extremely unlikely that she and her husband would have been warned of the coming famine if she had not shown hospitality to a weary traveler.

See how good God works and how he rewards those that delight in helping others?

You cannot beat God's giving.

Another lesson that we can learn from the Shunamite woman is to not put your trust in riches. No matter how much money she and her household had, the famine could have reduced them to poverty. This was a real possibility and was evident during the seven-year famine in Egypt that led to Pharaoh acquiring all the money, livestock, and land from the people (Genesis 47:13-25). The people spent all their money and traded all their belongings to acquire food, and eventually became Pharaoh's servants. By being generous with her wealth, the Shunamite woman was able to save her wealth and have her land restored to her household. Solomon, probably the richest man that ever lived, said: *"Those that trust in riches will wither, but the righteous will flourish like green leaves" (NRSV, Proverbs 11:28).*

It never pays to be stingy with your money. When you set other priorities and refrain from using your resources to bless others, you could very well be contributing to your own demise. Giving to others and organizations that exist to support those in need is insurance during times of economic hardship. This fact is supported by the scriptures below:

*"Tell those rich in this world's wealth to quit being so full of themselves and so obsessed with money, which is here today and gone tomorrow. Tell them to go after God, who piles on all the riches we could ever manage – to do good, to be rich in helping others, to be extravagantly generous. If they do that, they'll build a treasury that will last, gaining life that is truly life." (MSG, 1 Timothy 6:17 – 19)*

*"Some give freely, yet grow all the richer; others withhold what is due, and only suffer want. A generous person will be enriched, and one who gives water will get water." (NRSV, Proverbs 11:24-25)*

*"Those who are generous are blessed, for they share their bread with the poor." (NRSV, Proverbs 22:9)*

*"But a generous man devises generous things, and by his generosity he shall stand." (NKJV, Isaiah 32:8)*

**Chapter Summary**

You <u>should</u> continue to financially support your church and seek out ways to provide a blessing to others. Although tithing is an outdated practice not required by Christians, <u>you should not stop giving and supporting your church</u>. On the contrary, you should continue giving, but with the understanding that your offering is based on love and not from compulsion or fear of being cursed.

Determine the amount of your gift and give as often as you can. Do not feel ashamed of the amount of your gift, no matter how little it may be. The amount of your offering is not as important as your motive, and your motive should be love for God and your neighbor. Using your resources to help others is righteous behavior and is pleasing to God. You cannot say that you love God if you neglect those in need.

God will reward your giving. The blessings you have received from God should be reflected in your giving: <u>*"For unto whomsoever much is given, of him shall much be required"*</u> *(Luke 12:48)*. The more you give the more God will give you in return. Jesus said: <u>*"Give, and it will be given to you. A good measure, pressed down, shaken together and running over, will be poured in your lap; for the measure you give will be the measure you get back"*</u> *(NRSV, Luke 6:38)*.

Finally, let us remember Paul's words: <u>*"In all this I have given you an example that by such work we must support the weak, remembering the words of the Lord Jesus, for he himself said, 'It is more blessed to give than to receive'"*</u> *(NRSV, Acts 20:35)*.

# Chapter 6

# How Do You Financially Support a Church Organization?

The method to finance a religious organization first appeared in the Old Testament. Before I show you the specific details, let's establish the background. When Moses and the Israelites left Egypt, the Egyptians were anxious for them to leave and gave them parting gifts to hasten their departure: *"And the Egyptians were urgent upon the people, that they might send them out of the land in haste; for they said, We be all dead men...And the children of Israel did according to the word of Moses; and they borrowed of the Egyptians jewels of silver, and jewels of gold, and raiment: And the LORD gave the people favor in the sight of the Egyptians, so that they lent unto them such things as they required. And they spoiled the Egyptians"* *(Exodus 12:33-36)*. This was all part of God's plan, for He knew what the silver, gold, and raiment would be used for when He spoke with Abraham 400 years prior to the Jews leaving Egypt: *"And he said unto Abram, Know of a surety that thy seed shall be a stranger in a land that is not theirs, and shall serve them; and they shall afflict them four hundred years; And also that nation, whom they shall serve, will I judge: and afterward shall they come out with great substance"* *(Genesis 15:13-14)*.

While the Israelites were in the wilderness, God told Moses to build a sanctuary: *"And let them make me a sanctuary; that I may dwell among them"* *(Exodus 25:8)*.

Can you guess what was used as building material?

It was gold, silver, bronze, and fine linen along with a few other things: *"And this is the offering which ye shall take of them; gold, and silver, and brass, and blue, and purple, and scarlet, and fine linen"* *(Exodus 25:3-4)*.

Did you notice something?

God did not request anything the Israelites did not already possess! Much of the material used to build the temple were the items given to them by the Egyptians. Said differently, the things God asked for was not a burden on the Israelites to provide. In fact, God told Moses to only use what was willingly given from the heart: *"Speak unto the children of Israel, that they bring me an offering: of every man that giveth it **willingly** with his heart ye shall take my offering"* (Exodus 25:2), *"Take ye from among you an offering unto the LORD: whosoever is of a **willing** heart, let him bring it, an offering of the LORD; gold, and silver, and brass"* (Exodus 35:5), *"And they came, every one whose heart stirred him up, and every one whom his spirit made **willing**, and they brought the LORD's offering to the work of the tabernacle of the congregation, and for all his service, and for the holy garments. And they came, both men and women, as many as were **willing** hearted, and brought bracelets, and earrings, and rings, and tablets, all jewels of gold: and every man that offered an offering of gold unto the LORD"* (Exodus 35:21-22).

The keyword is willing. The Israelites gave a freewill offering. They were under no obligation to give, nor was there a curse for not giving. God took into consideration their current situation - former slaves wandering through the desert with only the resources they brought with them from Egypt. Despite the fact that contributions were only taken from those that gave willingly, more than enough was raised. In fact, Moses had to tell the people to stop giving: *"And they spake unto Moses, saying, The people bring much more than enough for the service of the work, which the LORD commanded to make. And Moses gave commandment, and they caused it to be proclaimed throughout the camp, saying, Let neither man nor woman make any more work for the offering of the sanctuary. So the people were restrained from bringing"* (Exodus 36:5-6). This should serve as a lesson that people will give generously when they are not forced. Contrast this with present-day churches where, no matter your situation (single parent, fixed income, unemployment, underemployment), you are commanded to give 10 percent of whatever income you receive.

The second time the Israelites were asked to contribute to the building of the temple was after the Babylonian captivity: *"Whosoever remaineth in any place where he sojourneth, let the men of his place help* *him with silver, and with gold, and with goods, and with beasts, beside the **freewill** offering for the house of God that is in Jerusalem...And all they that were about them strengthened their hands with vessels of silver, with gold, with goods, and with beasts, and with precious things, beside all that was **willingly** offered"* (Ezra 1:4, 6). Again, this was a freewill offering. The God of heaven and earth, who spoke the world into existence with the sound of His voice, does not want or desire anything from human beings that are not freely offered. God doesn't even need our praise. At one moment while Jesus was speaking to his disciples, He said if we withheld our praise the rocks would cry out: *"And when he was come nigh, even now at the descent of the mount of Olives, the whole multitude of the disciples began to rejoice and praise God with a loud voice for all the mighty works that they had seen; Saying, Blessed be the King that cometh in the name of the Lord: peace in heaven, and glory in the highest. And some of the Pharisees from among the multitude said unto him, Master, rebuke thy disciples. And he answered and said unto them, I tell you that, if these should hold their peace, the stones would immediately cry out" (Luke 19:37-40)*. God desires our praise; He does not command it.

In 2 Corinthians 9:7, Paul says: *"God loves a cheerful giver."* However, much is said prior to this verse regarding the attitude of giving. If the prior six verses are read in proper context, you will notice that Paul is talking about taking care of poor Christians: *"If I wrote any more on this relief offering for the poor Christians, I'd be repeating myself...Now I'm sending the brothers to make sure you're ready, as I said you would be, so my bragging won't turn out to be just so much hot air...So to make sure there will be no slipup, I've recruited these brothers as an advance team to get you and your promised offering all ready before I get there. I want you to have all the time you need to make this offering in your own way. I don't want anything forced or hurried at the last minute...I want each of you to take plenty of time to think it over, and make up your own mind what you will give. That will protect you against sob stories and arm-twisting" (MSG, 2 Corinthians 9:1-7)*.

Paul advises the Corinthians to collect the donations before he arrives. The Corinthians had already promised to provide funds for the poor so having it ready was not too much to ask. Taking this action would also improve appearances. It would show an act of generosity versus a grudging obligation. Paul says that each person should determine for themselves what they will give.

This is important!

Paul did not suggest a specified amount. He could have, but he didn't. Being one of the chief leaders of the early Christian church, Paul could have requested a specified amount. As a Pharisee familiar with the Jewish tithing system, Paul could have asked Christians to adopt principles of tithing and that everyone should give 10 percent of their earnings to take care of the poor and to fund the financial needs of the ministry. However, nowhere in the New Testament can you find where Paul or any other disciple called for receiving a specific amount from the congregation. <u>They understood that only God has the authority to command tithing, and they never had or were given permission to determine the amount people should give</u>. They also understood that because the tithe was holy to the Lord, it had well-defined parameters for its collection and use. Everything else given to support the ministry was considered a freewill offering, and its use was subject to their discretion.

Despite only being supported by freewill offerings, the early Christian church was quite successful in spreading the gospel across the world. Financing the expenses of the early Christian church did not require significant overhead as it does in many religious organizations today. Instead of meeting in synagogues and temples, the early Christians met in homes: *<u>"And when he had considered the thing, he came to the house of Mary the mother of John, whose surname was Mark; where many were gathered together praying"</u>* (Acts 12:12); *<u>"Also give my greetings to the church that meets in their home"</u>* (NLT, Romans 16:5); *<u>"The churches here in the province of Asia send greetings in the Lord, as do Aquila and Priscilla and all the others who gather in their home for church meetings"</u>* (NLT, 1 Corinthians 16:19).

The primary reason why Christians met in homes was to avoid religious persecution. But there is another reason to consider. The maintenance cost of a building would have diverted funds away from the poor, widows, and the needy. Taking care of people was far more important to the early Christians than maintaining buildings. By meeting in homes, overhead costs were kept low because someone already owned the home and was responsible for its upkeep.

This leads me to a very important point. God does not need, nor is He impressed by the elaborate buildings constructed today for church services. In fact, you cannot find anywhere in the Bible where God asked for an elaborate building! The first temple constructed by Moses was a tent.

It was David's desire to build God a temple: *"And David said to Solomon, My son, as for me, it was in my mind to build an house unto the name of the LORD my God"* (1 Chronicles 22:7). The Philistines had temples for their false gods. David lived in a palace, and he thought it was not right that God's dwelling place was a tent. God acknowledged David's desire, but he was not allowed to build the temple: *"Thou hast shed blood abundantly, and has made great wars: thou shalt not build an house unto my name, because thou hast shed much blood upon the earth in my sight"* (1 Chronicles 22:8). Solomon built the temple. However, there is no record that God was dissatisfied with the tent constructed by Moses. Although it was very beautiful, God was not overly concerned about the temple that Solomon built and allowed it to be destroyed and its artifacts stolen on multiple occasions: *"Nebuchadnezzar also carried of the vessels of the house of the LORD to Babylon, and put them in his temple at Babylon...And they burnt the house of God, and brake down the wall of Jerusalem, and burnt all the palaces thereof with fire, and destroyed all the goodly vessels thereof"* (2 Chronicles 36:7, 9); *"And Jesus went out, and departed from the temple: and his disciples came to him for to shew him the buildings of the temple. And Jesus said unto them, See ye not all these things? verily I say unto you, There shall not be left here one stone upon another, that shall not be thrown down"* (Matthew 24:1-2). It should be noted that the temple that Moses constructed was never destroyed; it was replaced by the one constructed by Solomon.

God is more concerned about building up people rather than buildings. Many churches today seem more concerned about acquiring a building rather than meeting the needs of its members. More time, money, and thought is given to the size, appearance, and location for a church than what is committed to looking after the needs of members or poor people in the surrounding community. This is hard to reconcile. While millions of dollars are set aside to build churches and provide for their maintenance, there are people in the congregation and community getting foreclosed, evicted, and are unable to pay for basic utilities or buy food. Somehow the building has become more important than the people.

The New Testament model of home-based ministries was very successful and smart. The early Christians met in homes, and this created a real sense of community, belonging, and intimacy with one another. By conducting services at someone's home, a new person that joins the congregation will not go unrecognized. If someone needs financial assistance, members can pool their resources together to help, whereas the money would otherwise go towards the cost of maintaining the building. By avoiding building expenses, the church can truly: _"Bear ye one another's burdens, and so fulfil the law of Christ"_ (Galatians 6:2). Presently, too much money is spent on things that are not important.

At some point, as the size of the ministry grows, it may become more practical to meet in a building instead of someone's home. When this occurs, instead of acquiring a large, expensive facility, build or rent several small, inexpensive facilities spread throughout the metropolitan area. The congregation size is purposefully kept small, and this fosters a better sense of community and belonging. Because the building is affordable, there is more money available for evangelism and outreach. By keeping overhead low, there is not a constant petition for money to maintain a large building.

Before a church moves into a larger building, the number of church services should expand. Instead of having only the traditional 11 AM service, an early morning service and an afternoon service should be added. This way, the building is fully utilized, and building expenses and the overall debt burden are distributed across several services. Reducing costs will ensure that money is available to help those in need. Additionally, the congregation size is kept small and manageable. Building expense should never hamper a church's ability to serve the poor.

Is God pleased with our worship when churches collectively spend millions of dollars on sound and lighting systems in order to enhance the worship experience, or are we just providing entertainment?

When Jesus was approached by the rich man that asked him: *"Good Master, what shall I do that I may inherit eternal life? (Mark 10:17)*, Jesus did not reply by saying to spend more money on church facilities to enhance worship. Jesus told him: *"Go thy way, sell whatsoever thou hast, and give to the poor" (Mark 10:21)*. Giving to the poor and taking care of those in need is the example that Jesus set and it was carried out by his disciples in the early Christian church. True worship is summed up in two commandments: *"Thou shalt love the Lord thy God with all thy heart, and with all thy soul, and with all thy mind. This is the first and great commandment. And the second is like unto it, Thou shalt love thy neighbor as thyself. On these two commandments hang all the law and the prophets" (Matthew 22:37-40)*. The first commandment shows us how to love God, and the second shows us how to love one another. Somehow, in the process of time, God's design has morphed into a system that looks nothing like the original.

While I must acknowledge that there are some churches that have outstanding ministries and meet the needs of the poor in their community and across the world, most fall short. The primary reason most churches are unable to meet the needs of the poor is too much of their resources are tied up in unnecessary church expense.

The early Christian church was not organized under a bloated conference system, as seen in many Christian denominations today, where more and more tithe payers are needed to sustain expanding staff and budgets. Those who served in the ministry, like Paul, worked for a living (Paul was a tentmaker, *Acts 18:3*) and received minimal support from the congregation. However, anyone who commits their lives to full-time ministry should be compensated by that ministry for their labor. Paul upheld this view when he quoted the Law of Moses: *"You shall not muzzle the ox while it treads out the corn" (Deuteronomy 25:4, 1 Corinthians 9:9)* and *"the laborer is worthy of his wages" (NKJV, 1 Timothy 5:18)*. To paraphrase, Paul says it is improper to prevent church leaders from receiving compensation when others are reaping the benefits of their labor. Having established this point, when Paul said that *"elders who rule well should be counted worthy of double honor"* (NKJV, 1 Timothy 5:17) he was not suggesting that the salary the pastor or anyone else receives from the church should make them the highest wage earner in the congregation!

The Bible says: *"For the love of money is the root of all evil"* (1 Timothy 6:10). It is the love of money that has turned many pastors into prosperity preachers, and this is why there is no shame in asking for a $65 million Gulfstream jet: *"And the Pharisees also, who were covetous, heard all these things: and they derided him. And he said unto them, Ye are they which justify yourselves before men; but God knoweth your hearts: for that which is highly esteemed among men is abomination in the sight of God"* (Luke 16:14-15).

A competent Pastor that does a good job managing the church's affairs should receive fair compensation. Just because a person is a minister does not mean that they should not be paid. I believe churches should pay their ministers a fair wage and also provide additional support, as needed. Let me illustrate what a fair salary and benefits package would look like in Atlanta, Georgia, for a congregation that has at least 100 adult wage-earning members. Obviously, the figures in the chart below will need to be adjusted for inflation and the church's location.

| Description | Monthly Avg. Cost | Annual Costs |
|---|---|---|
| Salary | $6,750 | $81,000 |
| Car Allowance | $300 | $3,600 |
| Health Insurance – Family Plan | $1,000 | $12,000 |
| Cell Phone, tablet, other device | $100 | $1,200 |
| **Total Compensation** | **$8,150** | **$97,800** |

The chart above breaks down the monthly and annual cost of providing one full-time pastor with a car, health insurance, cell phone and tablet, and $81,000 in annual salary. Depending on the congregation's size, membership demographic, and overall giving potential, this cost structure may be challenging and would need to be adjusted. For others, this plan is very affordable. Nonetheless, with the exception of prosperity preachers, this is an attractive benefits package for anyone seeking full-time employment in ministry. At the time of this writing, the United States Census Bureau data shows that the median household income in Georgia is $49,179. With approximately $98,000 in total compensation, a pastor could adequately support their family without holding a second job. More importantly, they can freely dedicate themselves to developing life-changing ministries for the church and the neighboring community.

**Chapter Summary**

The Old and New Testament show that people are very willing to give generously to support church activities. In fact, when a call was made for the people to give willingly, more was raised than was needed. This should serve as proof that a compulsory tithe is unnecessary. More faith is needed by pastors and church leadership in their member's willingness to give and financially support religious activities. Pastors and Christian denominations should resist the urge to determine for their members what percentage of their income is required to fund religious activities and pay for church expenses. This is unnecessary and inconsistent with biblical guidance.

# Other Books Written By

# Terrence Jameson

www.ingramcontent.com/pod-product-compliance
Lightning Source LLC
Chambersburg PA
CBHW061258040426
42444CB00010B/2415